[COMPANION ANIMAL]

ISBN: 978-1-933959-19-1

Cover art: Thordis Adalsteinsdottir, "Brown Cat in Studio," 2007, 30 X 45 cm, acrylic on canvas

Design & typsetting by HR Hegnauer
Text typset in Sabon

Litmus Press is a program of Ether Sea Projects, Inc., a 501(c)(3) non-profit literature and arts organization. Dedicated to supporting innovative, cross-genre writing, the press publishes the work of translators, poets, and other writers, and organizes public events in their support. We encourage interaction between poets and visual artists by featuring contemporary artworks on the covers of our books. By actualizing the potential linguistic, cultural, and political benefits of international literary exchange, we aim to ensure that our poetic communities remain open-minded and vital.

Litmus Press publications are made possible by public funds from the New York State Council on the Arts with the support of Governor Andrew Cuomo and the New York State Legislature. Additional support for Litmus Press comes from the Leslie Scalapino – O Books Fund, individual members and donors. All contributions are fully tax-deductible.

State of the Arts

NYSCA

Litmus Press
925 Bergen Street, Suite 405
Brooklyn, New York 112238
litmuspress.org

Distributed by Small Press Distribution
1341 Seventh Street
Berkeley, California 94710
spdbooks.org

Library of Congress Cataloging-in-Publication Data

Zurawski, Magdalena.
  [Poems. Selections]
  Companion Animal / by Magdalena Zurawski.
     pages cm
  Poems.
  ISBN 978-1-933959-19-1 (paperback : alk. paper)
  I. Title.
  PS3576.U543C66 2013
  811'.54--dc23

                   2013019256

[COMPANION ANIMAL]

MAGDALENA ZURAWSKI

LITMUS PRESS | 2015

life is these pronouns
PAUL BLACKBURN

Sound is the blood between me and you
WILD FLAG

FOR YOU

[ESSAY WITH DEAD FISH]

I'm wondering if a writer isn't a kind of failed magician. Or if it's an erroneous gesture for a reader or a writer to apply the kind of thinking required in the space of the book to a space outside of the book. What I mean is, a reader or a writer is praised for the correspondences she can make between things in the space of a book. The more unexpected relationships or links I can make between different ideas or objects in my book, the "smarter" I'll appear as a writer. The same goes for a reader. The person who can point out the most relationships between things, who can make the most meanings, is the best student. And maybe this is true in the game of reading. A magician, if I remember my Spicer correctly, is a person who does this in the world, in the world of real life. A magician creates correspondences between things that another person wouldn't necessarily see and that's where the magic comes from.

But I'm beginning to think that for a person to read the world in the same way that she reads a text is a kind of false or failed magic, if only because the world is not a sealed system the way a book is. A book is a limited set, whereas the world is infinite. We don't get the whole story when we are outside of a book, but the practice of reading books, especially if we are good at it, might make us confident enough to read the real this way. I think it gives us a false sense of control because the world is too big. Too many things remain outside our ken. So to create a narrative based on certain coincidences of experiences, to read life the way we read a book, seems to me, at least right now, emotionally dangerous. We can ascribe people and places too much significance.

Maybe I'm just feeling a victim of my own magic because the book I wrote before this book, the book I wrote before the one you are reading now, used so much of me as material for itself. The life of my early twenties is the furniture of that book, though most of the things that happen in that book never happened in real life. But inside the book, even though the things inside it never happened, the text inside the book started echoing so many parts of itself without me seeing it until it was all written and done. And so the book seemed so much smarter than I, who had written it. This made me think the book was filled with a special kind of magic. Everything corresponded in the book and so I began to believe the book could reach out beyond its pages and make meanings outside of itself. I thought the book could make meanings in my life.

A concrete example might help, especially since I am talking about a real problem, or at least I think I am talking about a real problem. I mean, I really had been stupid enough to think that the magic I had felt in the book was now making things, magical things, happen between me and a girl, who I met here outside of the book. And I like to think that the girl, too—even if only for a few minutes—I like to think that she, too, had thought for a moment there was a kind of magic between the two of us, if only because she had been caught by the book's magic, too, though she had only read the book but I had written it. Of course, the magic wouldn't have worked, if I hadn't written the book and she hadn't read it. I mean, she read the book and saw that I, or the character who might have been me, if it had been at all possible for the real me to make it into the book, this girl saw that I walked past her house in the book. And that fact I think seemed like a special kind of magic to us, a magic that meant something outside the book. We thought it was magic because inside the book I walk towards the river past the Portuguese bakery and if one is in Providence and walking towards the river past the Portuguese bakery, one would have to walk past this girl's house. So when she told me in real life that I walked right past her house in the book I could tell that both she and I thought that because I walked right past her house in the book that we both thought at least for a moment I should be walking not past but into her house in real life. But the problem with both of us thinking this about the book and how the book was making meanings in real life was that when I had lived in Providence there had been another Portuguese bakery on another corner that a person could also walk past in order to get to the river. But neither of us knew that at the time, though I think that the girl started to suspect something was wrong before I did.

And I don't think that the girl was smarter than I was, but maybe I was lonelier than she, and so sometimes I bent the magic inside the book to point at things outside the book to make them look as though I shouldn't be lonely and I should be together with this particular girl. For instance, one of the things I bent towards the girl outside the book had to do with a name inside the book. I had forgotten that one of the characters had the same name as this girl and I had only noticed the name again on the page once the book arrived on my doorstep from the publisher. And even though this name in the book was never meant to point to this particular girl outside the book, but was the name of someone who had once lived down the hall from me in real life many years ago, I still tried to force a kind of magic into this fact. I wanted to think that the book had always known that I would meet this girl and so my life was now going to change. And I wanted to believe this because the character in the book with the same name as the girl in real life speaks to me in a scene where we get drunk and I say "This river was made for us" and she says "I know. I know." And at the time I really wanted a place in the world for me and a girl and the river seemed just such a place, though I think I want all of that much less now. And I see now how wrong I was to think this way about the book and the girl. I was wrong to think about it this way because already the Portuguese bakery inside the book was different than the Portuguese bakery in real life, so it's possible that the river I walk to in the book is different than the river I walk to from the girl's house. You have to keep these things in mind after you write a book and then meet a girl.

What I mean is that after writing the book I began to believe there was the same kind of magic everywhere outside the book and this kind of thinking I know now is wrong. For me to know this, though, life had to correct my thinking, and show me that meanings in life were different than the meanings in books. And the way that life did this was to take me to the river with this girl. I arrived in Providence one day and tried to make things magical between us, and so I tried to go to the river with the girl. And it was as though life said, please, by all means, walk to the river with this girl, but I am afraid you will find no magic there. And it is only because I went to the river with the girl that afternoon, that I began to see there were perhaps moments when feelings coincided between people outside of books, but there was probably no magic between people in real life the way there's magic between words in books. I began to think this because when the girl and I arrived at the river we began to smell something terrible. Along the river we began to smell something like horse stables and fish markets and as we walked further down the path along the river we found ourselves ankle deep in mud and in the mud there were hundreds of dead fish. Dead silver fish in the mud. And that's when I saw that I was wrong about magic. Life had put the dead fish under my feet so that I would finally understand that I was not meant to go to the river with the girl in real life, even though there was a kind of magic in my book.

That's when I started to think that those things that happen outside of books aren't meant to be as magical as the things that happen to us inside of books. And I thought that maybe to try to make meanings in your life the way you would in a book is just the tic of a reader. And I thought maybe reading only works in books.

[THE FUTURE IS ONLY DEATH ABSTRACTED]

Most of the day I feel things. Nobody
pays me, I just do it. Water dripping
on the steel bowl rings out and I and
the dog on the couch have no God.

We have poetry,
which Jack gladly
gives up for a bowl of beef.

Not doing is a way of attaching
to your self again. To be lazy enough
to have thoughts creates no
surplus value. I don't have to be
anywhere in the morning and
will see the sunrise, will read
or not read. Tonight I open Taggart,
the book of John, where it is written,
"your soul is known by its dissatisfaction."

[YOU ARE MOSTLY BEAUTIFUL]

One sees little
in this light
that hasn't been
seen before. The shades

are up. One reminds
me of your mother.
That's not fair, you
say, but the world

makes pictures of
us all day long. When
I was green and
blossomed in the spring

I, too, gave people
rashes. Behind our
heads our bodies
are moving in front

of trees. Everyone
should stay connected,
but we don't.

[DISCLOSED LOCATION]

I feel broken at night groping
for a glass
there's a pill in the kitchen
to put me back
in the dark
on the radio
a woman says they're not going to burn
the Koran the general called
in the request and Laura's on the F
at Smith and 9th or maybe it's the G
meanwhile
I'm here on a street in a city
that does not appear in poetry.

I don't want the poem to be like life the poem should be real.

It's late and the dog
is on the red chair
           barking.

[BEDROOM SUITE]

[THE DUMB DOG COMES HOME]

I had by noon
gone down
to the bank.

Fool, I thought.
She could count me
out of my hands.

My face, at least,
will be my
own, I thought.

I will know me
by the mouth
that feeds her.

[STUPID IS AS STUPID FUCKS]

Fool, I said,
you made your
bed, now try
to fuck in it.

I lied to no one
in particular
to myself.

To my face I said,
you are still my own.

I lied alone in
bed next to her.

The dog, now
dead, asleep
at my feet.

[WE HAVE NO WORDS]

My face quietly
stands in place
of itself.

The television,

a light against
our bodies, a nothing
instead of the dark.
          No bite,
          no bark.

[EVENING SHIFT]

One to thirty
black fleas and
T.V. is another
word for let's
not fuck. Again
no luck. Men

on the street
watch me walk
the blind
dog in fog—

(watch
the raccoon
bathe in moon-
light.)

[UNLUCKY PIERRE]

A small dog came
into bed and
slept across the
body's legs.

Elsewhere, covered
in a sheet, she
breathed herself away
from me.

For my own
sake I kept
a small face.
A bony place
with a thin
set of lips.

(I managed
a nervous
hand across
the head.)

[WHAT CAN'T BE FIXED CAN BE PROLONGED]

I heard that
when they found
my face in
the freezer,
she was in the dark

watching football. I heard
that I must have been out
walking

the dog, that
I might have been dead
asleep.

[IF A FACE BARKS, WHO CAN HEAR IT?]

There is no
reason to say
anything except

I did not say it

then. I did
not, even when
turned away
from the mirror,

love you.

[CLARIFICATION]

When I
say *We*
I mean
the dog
and me.
Not *We* (the people) or
We (my girl
and me.)

We is
my dog
and me.

FEBRUARY 13, 2012

Dear Buuck—

The problem is both that poetry seems to do nothing to make things better in any material way, and yet we can't stop ourselves from writing it. We need it and don't even know why. And even if poetry is just a kind of astrology through which we begin to dream that we can be a *we*, it seems we've been dreaming a long time, and, still, you and I wake up every morning alone with a pencil in hand. And what would I do with *you* and *you* and *you*, if we became a *we*? You said the first step to utopia is breathing, so poetry is that first step, but it seems none of us trust that answer—instead we talk about overturning cop cars.

I don't know if I believe in anything. Not *you*, or *we*, but then *I* feel so little, so unbelievable, too. And then I wake up and need to write poems and suddenly I feel like I'm not dying anymore.

Yours,

—M

P.S. If the cops lock Anne up, I promise to take care of Hazel.

[PENCILS WOULD LAY BRICKS]

money
doesn't
change
matter
only
rearranges
matters
words
matter
only
betray
forms
of
thinking
wishful
thinking
maybe
I
wish
matters
would
change
words
from
thought
forms
to
hard
nickel

matter
or
maybe
I
wish
words
could
change
matters
not
just
think
about
how
wrongly
love
and
money
move
through
this
world
if
words
could
push
back
against
this
world
which

presses
down
so
hard
on
our
little
words
poetry
would
be
another
matter
not
as
another
form
of
matter
not
any
kind
of
money
but
poetry
would
be
our
own
thoughts

real
and
pressing
like
the
hand
of
our
dreams
rearranging
matters
the
things
that
matter
as
worlds
not
words
poetry
would
let
us
call
our
world
into
being
could
make
things

not
just
disclose
them
and
I
could
finally
stop
saying
every
time
I
looked
at
this
world, WE COULD HAVE IMAGINED ANYTHING AND
    THIS IS ALL WE CAME UP WITH
I
could
stop
reading
Lukács
and
say, IN THE BEGINNING THERE WAS THE WORD
and
it
would
mean
something.

[THE RAIN IS HOW WE LIVE IN IT]

I am life breathing is
life don't forget
the loose green
twitch of plants. Plants destroy

flesh stand here
long enough and
the vines choke you.
'Who's there?' 'Speak!'

Fred says, 'Life
escapes.' I am life
and what can't fall
in line comes out

sideways. This is
political theory.

[TWO POETS TAKE A NAP]

Let's call this
MACHINE
GUN
    though
we both know it's
a pillow.

[You place your head to rest
alongside mine.
It's not very long
before one of us is gone.]

[IT'S TIME TO HEAR THE MUSIC ON THE WALL]

I read that
only if we
abide by
every sensation
will we break
into light-

houses and
live as if
we belonged.
I want to
believe it,
so I do.

[DOG IS A WAY OF THINKING]

My language, which likes
to prove I am not

alone, wants
to talk to me again
today. It's

telling me, Don't
forget: you want
to be less like Homer and
not at all like Milton, but
more like your dog. Your
dog, my language
says, knows things are
there, doesn't want
blindness to see
a world, only a nose
to know what's
knocking now, who's on
her way home. There's
no yesterday.

Your dog, if he could
talk, my language tells
me, would, every
day, like a radio,
catch an air wave and
say, "Today…"

[MONEY IS THE FORM OF MY REGRET]

Beginning with some words taken from Aaron Kunin

What is mine
is not yours unless
you take it.

What I mean is
every dollar
hides a weeping
pair of genitals.

(If you can't say sorry
you aren't sorry.)

I am sorry that
I gave you my money. I am
sorry that you took
my money and gave it
to your brother.

(You never put out.)

What I mean is
when I said "Marco"
you didn't say "Polo." You
said my last name
could get us a longer
line of credit.

I wish I hadn't had
a last name. I wish
I had traded my
last name for 1,000 poems
and a blow job.

But you would have
taken my poems from me
every night when you came
home with your money
in your pockets.

I would have cursed
you for taking my poems
instead of me.

(I would have wanted
some of your money.)

[POST THIS ON YOUR WALL TO KEEP OTHERS INFORMED]

Some light breaks thick
with green

hits the trailer where a mop
hangs from a limb, a branch not far
from the door. Not all

of us are permitted
to see. My house
has windows. On the street

the neighbor sees us,
says, *Look at the black
one*, pointing at

the pug. I let the pug
closer. *He won't bite, will he?*
No, I say, *she's a lover. It's*

*the white one you've
got to watch.*

[SMELLS LIKE MIDDLE-AGED SPIRIT]

We who loafe and loiter still show
up to work on time. It's the iron
in irony and no longer funny.

For instance, if you take
a poll you'll find most
anyone will trade a seat

at the table for a table. This
desire is no longer limited
to western philosophers

trying to prove shit. The beauty of
it is history herself, her elasticity
of form. She has left each of us

in our own way wanting
the feel of a new shirt,
no matter how uncool.

[YOUR CART IS EMPTY]

skinny boys
were made
for clothes
in which
others feel
mostly terrible
even when
naked God
is a word
for the bell
we ring
for liberty
makes a
sound to
say there's
plenty of
corn syrup
in the cotton
candy but
just for me

[SUDDENLY VECTORS SHIFT]

To look up there a sky
seems no reason of God and

here in what's mostly me
it's dumb in my soul. I hear
nothing. Even when hard

of cash I never say please,
thanks, amen. And when
misery falls on me I don't

lean on a lord or king, but
curse bankers, curse this or
that girl. I never sound

"O Christ, O Child, whither
should I go?" But this one
day the poem went up.

Stacy was dead and God
seemed a little word for that.

[IT'S HARD TO KNOW WHAT I AM THINKING
WHEN I AM THINKING]

Sometimes
a squirrel hangs
over me
in sleep
as I dream
a squirrel hangs
over me
in sleep.
A doctor stands
at arm's
length long
enough to say
it's been said
before. It has
been said before.
So little
is answered
at arm's length. I wake up
thinking do I
really need arms?

I'd like
to keep
the squirrels, though,
and the trees
at night are
maybe enough
for poetry.

[HOW I MADE MY MOTHER GASP]

And in the
violence
and fever
of being
a creature
of thumbs I thought
suddenly to
gasp instead of
grasp. I thought to
gasp in form could
change me from a
creature of digits
to one of breath. This
thought made my mother
gasp and though I had
a sense that life even
for a creature of grasp
was still mostly in the
gasp what I didn't know
was that to be a creature
of gasp was to sense the
violence and the fever
of being a creature of
grasp and to gasp about it.

[PILLOWS TALK]

Your name
sounds against
my face. I feel
it but it doesn't
bring you.

You slip from
your lips then
slip away.

[INTERPRETATIVE OXFORD]

Why to cheat *on*? Strange preposition.
The OED suggests it's an inversion
of an oath. A person pledges fidelity
with a hand *on* (a bible, etc.). Then
where does the hand go?

[A FACE]

I turned to
where everything blew. There
wind blew into
a spoon. I turned
with the wind and
faced the spoon.

There where
in the spoon
I faced my face I
split with sight
and laughed—a firefly
in a jar.

[SOME PLURALS ARE PERSONAL]

for Michelle

They filled
every hollow space
with debt and

made us trip
over facts of their own
devising.

At night we sat alone,
together in the light
of the TV, prattling,
"Lord, what will
become of me?"

[THE MOUTH IS AN ENTRANCE]

Through a strange
mishap
    I lost all
     my content

and spent many years
in a book
    with the hope I could put a word

inside me
again.

    I needed something to say.

One night I drove across the bridges

but arrived too late

to sleep
    next to you.

Instead,
I sat on the wooden chair.

No matter,
you greeted me
     in the morning.

I seemed to be someone
you could know.

[SO LITTLE]

really has happened.
I just want
some time to think

about nothing—Ajax
in his fury
saw, for instance,
two suns and
a double Thebes. How

dangerous, she said,
is it to have

an imagination. I heard it
as a question, so I said,
more dangerous, I think,
not to have.

Now, in my living, God rises
each day, a ghost
in my skin, a burn.

[MODERN LANGUAGE ASSOCIATION]

We were delayed
for nearly
an hour.

Someone threw
a body on
the tracks before

we could
reach
Providence.

[ASPHALT]

Dogs piss or
don't piss.

Kids argue
about Thoreau. Argue
yes or no
on the machine
of state. I'm

not impartial. I want
my house HERE.
A lot with sunshine.

Neighbor says
the old man won't
sell to whites. Says anyhow
shoes on a line
mean drugs. Points up. No I say
they mean I was
here. I saw it
on TV. Another

neighbor interrupts. Says

eventually everybody
needs money.

[THE MONKEY]

The monkey survived, and I
took care of him. Morning
apples and evening crusts.

Long after you
denied me, he
thrived. I and
the monkey, not
you, but I and
the monkey survived.

[FLIP IT]

after Eileen

Sometimes
you're just
glad you're
happening. It
makes no
sense. The
sky is
falling and
they've trade-
marked the
sun. Still
I feel
it on
my face
and like
it. I know,
it's stupid.

[INVITATION TO A MARXIST LESBIAN PARTY]

Dear Marge,
Hello.

Poetry
is only
a form
of money,
if you're
an ass-
hole.

[#UNOCCUPIED]

After everyone stops
smoking the Ovid
it gets ugly to be alive.

The dead refuse us and
instead someone I know turns over
a police car and nothing

happens anymore not even
my face so empty and
too full of other people's

meanings.

I was bored and you
were bored, remember?

We dreamed of
leaving our heads
without a single
noun in them.

[A CONGRESSMAN NAMED WIENER RESIGNED TODAY]

Progress isn't
the way forward
in love or politics. Humiliation
makes the Spring

sad and wet, not
hot. At night
I see your face
in the screen. Can't

hear your voice.
Silence makes it
half a picture, a weak
metaphor. I could

send you a shot
of my hardon,
but I don't want
you to have me

so easily. Humiliation
isn't progress. I want
a love letter. I want
elegant syntax produced

by profound feeling,
but will settle for
profound feeling
produced by elegant

syntax. Humiliation
is sad and wet,
but not demanding.
There's just enough

food in the fridge
to keep a bachelor alive
for 30 days. I want
to lose enough

weight, so that you
can't know me
when you walk through
the door. Still, when

I jerk off, I see
your mouth silent
and it's moving.

[EROS, AIRING ITS BURN]

We were not that far from what had been
given us to call home. I couldn't sleep and was searching
for someone else's words in a book, something
that could tell you what you had done to me
because my words had always failed.
"What were you thinking?" "Nothing." You were
thinking *Nothing*. To say anything was impossible,
so I said, "Look, there are insects

in the trees. There's an owl on the telephone
wire." Now alone with the dog who sleeps
with his legs up, I find, "Willingly, I had given
my hand. Your flesh had fallen away."

[A HORIZON IS A LINE YOU CAN'T CROSS]

for Michael Gizzi

Outside of light a face can't find
itself. A little dog leads with
his snout. Somewhere behind us there's
laughter in a circle we don't
belong to – a score of ghosts who've
issued us no invitation

yet. What happened earlier is
just a little bit always happening. I remember
his voice thick and deep not tired,
like my own shadow can't escape me. What moves
my hand to the page can't make a world

a word. Sometimes the voices of my heroes
recede into the background – I
have to squint to hear them. Comments and
birds flit through the air speaking up
but not clearly. Warbled. *Michael
is dead.* The dead are those

who shouldn't have died, those who follow
you home at night. The dead are knocking, are knocking
you over with wind. They draw no
syllables. They are on the horizon,
broken like an uncle after

Sunday dinner. The roses are just bushes.
Don't disturb the birds: they're crying.

[IF THE WATER'S COLD A PERSON FINDS SOMETHING ELSE TO DO BESIDES SWIM]

I sang fully, sang
carefully though no
one was listening.
I was listening,
and the singing was
not without spirit.
You know, in the sun-
light I could feel the
feeling of not be-
ing a half, but rath-
er of having this
face to look into.
There was a dire, I
mean, a direction.

I was looking in
without reflecting,
was not 'what am,' or
'why,' etcetera
but I felt myself
and was not far and
lonesome but bishop
to myself so with-
out hat, but appoint-
ed, official. I
was for once all real,
you know?

[ESSAY WITH DEAD BIRD]

That morning when I walked passed the glass door I saw the body of a bird. It lay on its back, feet in the air. It resembled something like a parakeet crossed with a sparrow, but I didn't know a name for it. Its body was whole and unravished, a museum specimen. The sight of the bird woke a pleasant sorrow in me. This, I thought, was the feeling people had when they saw Ophelia dead in the water. I called Gina over and pointed my finger at the small body on the other side of the glass. She gasped quietly. It must have mistaken the clear door for air, she said.

Yes, I thought. We had inadvertently killed it. We had removed the ugly drape our landlord had used to cover the glass. I turned to Gina and said, "I'll clean it up later." I put the drape back in its place and got dressed for work.

All day I thought about the bird. I thought about how its dead body didn't disgust me, but only made me sad. Once there had been a dead rat in the basement and another time a dead raccoon in the yard. Neither animal's death made me sad. I never saw either carcass because I hadn't come upon the animals myself and later refused to look at them. In both cases friends came and took them away. The bird, though, I wanted to remove myself. This I knew was only because the bird was beautiful. For a moment it made me mistrustful of myself. After class I asked three of my students, if they thought it appropriate to feel sorrow for something dead simply because it was beautiful. All three listened seriously, but gave no answer. Walking home, I thought, it was unfair of me to ask my students such questions, even if I was the creative writing professor.

Recently some graduate students had told me that "bird" was a word too often used in poetry and should be avoided. I had had birds in many of my early poems, but had lately stopped putting them in my work. I had made this choice, however, before the graduate students had warned me. On my walk I tried to remember Spicer's poem about the birds in the Rare Book Room. Later I found the lines. I had thought they were in the "Imaginary Elegies," but they were in "Song for Bird and Myself": "Once two birds got into the Rare Book Room. / Miss Swift said, / Don't / Call a custodian / Put crumbs on the outside of the window / Let them / Come outside." And then a few lines later "But Miss Swift went to lunch. They / Called a custodian. / Four came. / Armed like Myrmidons, they / Killed the birds. / Miss Munsterberg / Who was the first / American translator of Rilke / Said / 'Suppose one of them / Had been the Holy Ghost.'" I had remembered the part about the Holy Ghost, but had thought Miss Munsterberg had been a Dickinson scholar, not a Rilke translator. Perhaps we, too, had killed the Holy Ghost as it tried to enter our house.

After I took the dogs out, I got a small shovel and a paper bag. I gently put the bird in the bag and folded the paper, making the bag not much larger than the bird. I had assumed at first that I would put the bag in the trash, but now with the bird in it, I thought it not right. I went out back and dug a small hole at the end of the yard. I placed the bag in it and covered it with dirt. Afraid it wasn't deep enough, I found a bag of leftover potting soil and poured it on top of the small grave. Now, when I look out the window from where I write, I can see the mound.

[ON DUTIES]

for Conrad

When I was a public
property the librarian
shooed the homeless
from my rib cage. She said,
"This is not a shelter." I said,
"But I am a public

property." "Who said
that?" the librarian said. I didn't
say anything. Instead,

Ben Franklin showed
her the door and invited
the Philadelphians inside.
Freely they inhabited me, living
and reading indoors.

[PARADISE WAS A GATED COMMUNITY]

Why can't we
begin to live forever together
before we die?

The after-life,
may never
pay out. Besides,

we have the world's
most perfect climate,
though we've missed

the Fall. Some
say it's coming. You
can smell it hanging

in the air. The light,
too, has changed and I
hear an urgency

in my voice. Life, it
seems, is fit to fuck us
at any moment.

[A SPACE FOR A CHORUS COMES WITH SUNLIGHT]

Who in winter might
remember spring
can help us escape.

What I make
is easy to forget.

Grey words break, but
the dog with his ears shorn
appears like a lamb.

[ALWAYS HISTORICIZE: FRANKLIN REMIX]

A penny saved
isn't worth
the price of
its production.

[DISTRESSED PROPERTY]

Poetry,
let's divide
the shares.
Let's cut
my face
in two.
One part
for you.
One part
for the
hard money.

Evenings I
after five
can sing
without a
care at
underthemoneytree.com. There
my face
can't split.

(I'm always where
no one listens.)

[STORM WATCH]

This weather comes
too soon—

Don't hesitate to take
a broom to it. Insects
get everywhere.

The old man's
troubled by the worms and the dog

won't take his pill.

[DOMESTIC SCENE REVISED]

All night the moths thrash against the glass.
It bothers the pug. She growls and
we don't get much wink. We hold
hands in half-sleep. The boy dog
doesn't mind the noise. Something
keeps him alive in his dream—the chase.

(In writing I always feel like a man but not

in the way that I feel things. I think I feel things
as a girl should feel things. I want to feel like a man
in the way I write things—I catch myself always trying to catch
a "man's" sound. This poem is no exception.)

[A CRAWL SPACE IS NOT A FOUNDATION]

The entrance of a new old couch
might change the feelings
in the house. You've fallen

into a dark pool. Me, I'm a dumb spouse, a quiet fool
taken once by a rat, twice nightly by mice. Wood roaches, grass-
hoppers creep in the door. The dog won't

ignore such presences. Will piss
next to his bowl. I, for the feeling
of control, will kill with bare hands
smaller things. A storm leaks in

to rot the sill. I'll not think to eat
breakfast. Coffee is too much, is
that thing that's not enough.

[ASK STUDENTS TO SAY THEIR NAMES]

I, too, can
in the dark
see things.

(A great light, for instance.)

It does
not get
us any-
where

except here

where we can
imagine beauty.
Restrict yourself

to the minute. Let
words fall across the page—

[KADDISH]

For God
there is nothing
more important
than sound.

To sit
soundless
in his house
is to have
lived all wrong
all along.

Poets belong
to the tempo
of that house.
Stacy and Uncle Mike
play there.

And sometimes on the sea there's room to speak
and I pretend to hear all three of them.

[FINAL VALENTINE]

I felt sure
that together you
and I might be an example
of something beautiful
and on a spring
day that was really only
mid-February we celebrated ourselves
too soon. I
walked into a barn
and let the baby goats suck
my fingers until
they bled. It's instinct
to cry when the skin
breaks. You stared
with the other agricultural
tourists who had also assented
to the liability clause.
If the chickens
knew anything, they didn't say. A cow
named Blackie
followed the children
like a dog. Later
they ate him.

[FOR GODFREY]

I'm on, John. I stole
your town of nouns.

My mouth's a peach.
It routs and spits

your pits, so keep
it quip. John, you're on

the stairs. It's night.
you descend in yellow

light. You know the sound
is ground. Not God up

and free but alphabet fuzz,
a fly for buzz, a needle

in the radio. You know
the way, the way I
want to know.

[RESEMBLANCE]

I am a lot like my father. He wants people around him, but
he doesn't want to talk to them. I want books around me,
but I don't want to read them. At parties I have nothing to
say. Before I arrive, I hope that others have brought their
instruments.

[FREE JOY WITH FRANK LIMA]

I think
I am
staying
in. It's

Friday. The poets
are gone.

I'm going to drop
quarters on the floor
like there's no
meters.

[

Now that I'm old
it's hard to get any

writing done. Every
day I'm busy

thinking how
poetry might

not mean
anything. And I've

got to vacuum, feed
the dogs, and teach

kids to care about
poetry. Today one

asked me how we could
get poetry its *power*

back. *What power
has poetry ever had,*

I thought and, *look around, kid, what power
is worth having?* But instead

I said, *maybe that's
not the way to think*

about it. I don't know
how to think about it.

I don't want to disappoint anyone.

When I was young
I learned that poetry

was *a little light*
in all that darkness.

I don't want to stub it out.

DEAR READER,

This book began some time in 2009 with a phone call from my friend CAConrad. That evening I confessed a fear to him. Since the completion of my first book, a novel published in 2008, I was scared to write, but daily I felt displaced from myself because I wasn't writing. I worried that I did not have another book in me and I worried that after working in prose for several years I no longer knew how to write poems, and so I avoided sitting down and writing. I was in graduate school and had plenty of "critical work" to do, but that did not feel like my real work, like my real being. The academic work helped me understand what it meant to be an American writing in the 21st century a little better, but it didn't help me write. In fact, it helped me to continually think about all of the problems of attempting to write something now, about poetry's relevancy etc. in endless answer-less circles.

Conrad in a great act of friendship immediately devised a ritual to help me. It was a simple one. I was to pull seven books of poetry I loved from my shelves and each evening read a little from each of them, then write in my notebook for twenty minutes. At least once a week I was to send him a new poem via email. He watched over me until the training wheels were off, until I had something like a habit.

The first poems were small poems, poems by someone who got "jilted" and now trusted the company of her dog most. The content was embarrassing enough, but I hadn't written anything in a while, so I wasn't going to get picky, and I hadn't ever written small, "flat" poems before. That was interesting to me. Anyhow, that's where the title *Companion Animal* came from. Obvious enough. Over the course of writing this book the work unbeknownst to me began to expand the meaning of the title. Life had begun to expand the poems. Two poet-friends died, other friends were losing their jobs or worrying about losing their jobs, some were worrying about getting jobs (myself included), some were worrying about losing their homes, everyone was broke or knee-deep in debt or feeling guilty about not being broke and knee-deep in debt while everyone else was broke and knee-deep in debt. Love and money and everything in between got suddenly *precarious*, to use a perhaps over-used term. So the poems became about *all that* and wondering what poetry could do with or for or around *all that*. Not sure there's an answer, but there are these poems.

In a small, quiet way, then, these poems feel an allegiance with others elsewhere, Demented Panda and Koki, and Anne Boyer to name a few. Many people also helped these poems come into being: Michelle Koerner, the world's greatest lounge chair player; Jack, my constant four-legged writing companion; the poets of Durham, NC; the members of the Highland-Maynard compound; the poets of Naropa, Summer 2012, Week 1; Gina, Jack, and Ava, who make daily life less precarious; and, of course, CAConrad, who jumpstarted everything.

Many friends helped these poems into the world. Much gratitude to Fred Moten and Joe Donahue for publishing some of these poems as a chapbook from Three Count Pour. And thanks to Gina Abelkop, Sue Landers, Lily Brown, and Joseph Massey for publishing some of this work online. Thanks to the editors of *Abraham Lincoln*, *The Denver Quarterly*, *Lit*, and *Oxford American*, who published some of these works. And a very special thanks for all the hard work that Tracy, Ashley, erica, and H.R. put into making this little book happen.

—MZ
Athens, 2015

ABOUT THE AUTHOR

Magdalena Zurawski is the author of *The Bruise* (FC2, 2008). She teaches literature and creative writing at the University of Georgia. She lives in Athens (Georgia).

green
press
INITIATIVE

Litmus Press is committed to preserving ancient forests and natural resources. We elected to print this title on 30% post consumer recycled paper, processed chlorine free. As a result, for this printing, we have saved:

2 Trees (40' tall and 6-8" diameter)
926 Gallons of Wastewater
1 million BTU's of Total Energy
61 Pounds of Solid Waste
170 Pounds of Greenhouse Gases

Litmus Press made this paper choice because our printer, Thomson-Shore, Inc., is a member of Green Press Initiative, a nonprofit program dedicated to supporting authors, publishers, and suppliers in their efforts to reduce their use of fiber obtained from endangered forests.

For more information, visit www.greenpressinitiative.org.

Environmental impact estimates were made using the Environmental Defense Paper Calculator. For more information visit: www.papercalculator.org.